SPIT AND PHLEGM!

T0014582

By Anthony Capicola

Gareth Stevens
PUBLISHING

Please visit our website, www.garethstevens.com. For a free color catalog of all our high-quality books, call toll free 1-800-542-2595 or fax 1-877-542-2596.

Cataloging-in-Publication Data

Names: Capicola, Anthony.
Title: Spit and phlegm! / Anthony Capicola.
Description: New York : Gareth Stevens Publishing, 2018. | Series: Your body at its grossest | Includes index.
Identifiers: ISBN 9781482464726 (pbk.) | ISBN 9781482464740 (library bound) | ISBN 9781482464733 (6 pack)
Subjects: LCSH: Saliva–Juvenile literature. | Mucus–Juvenile literature.
Classification: LCC QP191.C37 2018 | DDC 612.3'13–dc23

Published in 2018 by
Gareth Stevens Publishing
111 East 14th Street, Suite 349
New York, NY 10003

Designer: Sarah Liddell
Editor: Ryan Nagelhout

Photo credits: Cover, p. 1 (girl) wavebreakmedia/Shutterstock.com; cover, p. 1 (background) GooDween123/Shutterstock.com; background gradient used throughout rubikscubefreak/ Shutterstock.com; background bubbles used throughout ISebyl/Shutterstock.com; p. 5 stickasa/ Shutterstock.com; p. 7 Pawel Graczyk/Shutterstock.com; p. 9 sanjayart/Shutterstock.com; p. 11 sabza/Shutterstock.com; p. 13 Littlekidmoment/Shutterstock.com; p. 15 Lapina/ Shutterstock.com; p. 17 DigitalFabiani/Shutterstock.com; p. 19 Oksana Mizina/Shutterstock.com; p. 21 jarabee123/Shutterstock.com.

Printed in China

CPSIA compliance information: Batch #CS17GS: For further information contact Gareth Stevens, New York, New York at 1-800-542-2595.

CONTENTS

Boldface words appear in the glossary.

Waking Up Gross

You wake up one morning and don't feel well. Your throat is scratchy, and your nose starts to run. Oh no, you're sick! Better grab the **tissues**, because you'll be dealing with a lot of spit and phlegm (FLEHM) over the next few days!

Chew on This

Spit and phlegm are totally natural things the body makes. "Spit" is another word for saliva (suh-LY-vuh). It's made in the mouth. "Phlegm" is another word for mucus (MYOO-kuhs). It's made by body parts in the mouth, nose, throat, and lungs.

PHLEGM MADE IN THE MOUTH, NOSE, THROAT, AND LUNGS

SPIT MADE IN THE MOUTH

7

From the Glands

Saliva is made in body parts called glands. There are three main pairs of salivary glands, or glands that make saliva. A healthy person's salivary glands make about 2 to 4 pints (1 to 2 L) of saliva per day!

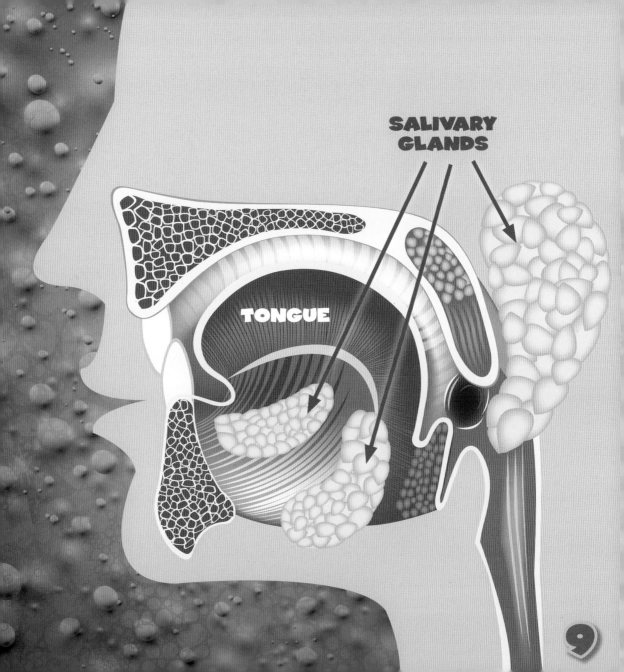

SALIVARY GLANDS

TONGUE

9

What It Does

Saliva is mostly water, but helps you in many ways. First, it helps you eat! Saliva makes food wet so it's easier to swallow. Saliva also has **enzymes**. These enzymes help break down food. This is the first step in **digestion**.

Taste and Protect

Saliva also helps you taste food! Your tongue needs to be wet to taste food. Without saliva, your **taste buds** don't work! Saliva also helps keep your mouth clean and fights **germs**. It even helps your teeth stay strong!

WHAT DOES SALIVA DO?

FIGHTS GERMS

HELPS TASTE FOOD

KEEPS YOUR MOUTH WET

BREAKS DOWN FOOD

BLOCKS BAD BREATH

KEEPS TEETH SAFE

Too Much Spit!

Sometimes the body makes too much saliva. Other times, a person doesn't have enough saliva. Since saliva is mostly made of water, it's important to drink lots of water to help your body make it!

From the Nose

Mucus is made to keep your throat and nose wet. The mucus called phlegm is found in the nose and throat. It's different from spit. It drips into your throat from the back of your nose. It traps germs, dust, and pollen and keeps them out of your lungs.

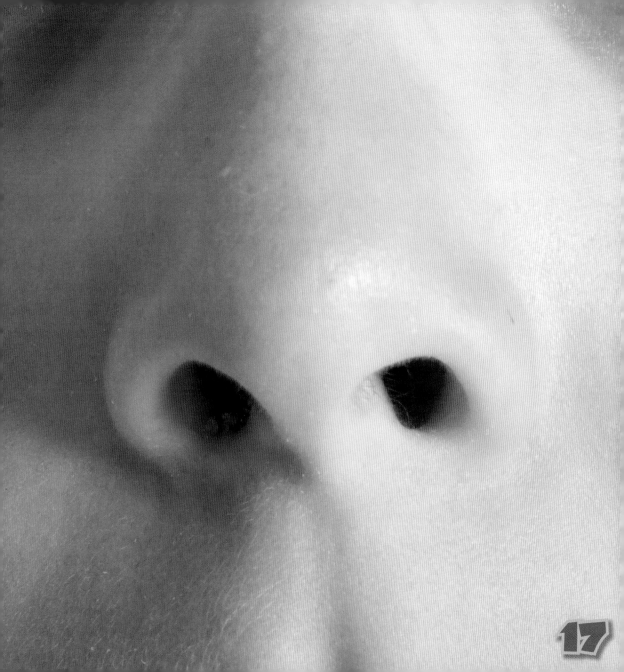

17

Turning Colors

There's more phlegm in your throat when you're sick. The body makes more mucus when it's fighting a cold or the flu. And mucus can turn colors! When you get sick, clear mucus gets thicker and becomes yellow or green.

Get It Out!

When you're sick, you sometimes have to get rid of all that extra phlegm! If it gets in your mouth, make sure you spit it into a tissue. And go see a doctor. They can give you **medicine** so you can get better!

GLOSSARY

digestion: the act of breaking down food inside the body so that the body can use it

enzyme: matter made in the body that helps certain actions necessary for life to occur

germ: a tiny living thing that can cause sickness

medicine: a drug taken to make a sick person well

taste bud: a body part on the surface of the tongue that helps recognize taste

tissue: thin paper used for blowing the nose

FOR MORE INFORMATION

BOOKS

Larsen, C. S. *Crust & Spray: Gross Stuff in Your Eyes, Ears, Nose, and Throat.* Minneapolis, MN: Millbrook Press, 2010.

McDonald, Megan. *Stink-O-Pedia. Volume 2: More Stink-y Stuff from A to Z.* Somerville, MA: Candlewick Press, 2010.

WEBSITES

The Immune System
cyh.com/HealthTopics/HealthTopicDetailsKids. aspx?p=335&np=152&id=2402
Learn more about how mucus helps the body stay healthy on this site.

What's Spit?
kidshealth.org/en/kids/spit.html
Find out more about what spit does here.

INDEX